Quick & easy

Goldfish
Care

T.F.H. Publications
One TFH Plaza
Third and Union Avenues
Neptune City, NJ 07753

This book has been published with the intent to provide accurate and authoritative information in regard to the subject matter within. While every precaution has been taken in preparation of this book, the publisher and author assume no responsibility for errors or omissions. Neither is any liability assumed for damages resulting from the use of the information herein.

ISBN 0-7938-1041-8

www.tfh.com

Table
of Contents

Goldfish
Basics

oldfish have been with us for over a thousand years. The typical goldfish as we know it today does not occur in the wild but is thought to have first been bred by the Chinese from natural mutations of the wild goldfish, a popular food fish. The original wild variety of goldfish still exists in rivers, lakes, and sluggish streams of its native China, where its somber olive color blends in with murky waters, providing the fish with excellent camouflage. Even today, the young of most domestic goldfish varieties start life with the same somber coloring, only attaining the peak of their characteristic golden tones when they are about a year old.

From China to Europe

While goldfish were mentioned in Chinese poetry as early as 800 AD, it is believed that they did not arrive in Europe until about 1600, when they were frequently mentioned by European authors of that era.

Because of their beautiful coloring and often extreme hardiness, goldfish have become one of the most popular pets in the world. So popular are they that they still are given away at carnivals and circuses in games of chance! Until recently, a spherical or drum-shaped bowl containing a couple of miserable-looking goldfish was a common feature in many homes. Unfortunately for their well-intentioned keepers, however, the very shape of the bowl provided an insufficient surface area for the absorption of oxygen from the air and the passage of carbon dioxide into the air. This led to poor water conditions and very lethargic goldfish often on the verge of death. Fortunately, the old fishbowl concept of keeping is almost a thing of the past today, and goldfish now regularly are being displayed in rectangular aquaria with large surface areas, usually augmented by filters and air pumps.

External Features

The wild goldfish and its domesticated descendants belong to the carp family, Cyprinidae, and are part of the species called *Carassius auratus*, closely related to the Crucian carp, *Carassius carassius*. Most carp possess barbels on their lips, but in the case of goldfish and Crucian carp the barbels are absent. Wild goldfish are fairly deep-bodied fish with a gently curved back. The dorsal fin has a long base and contains some 15 to 19 branched rays and a strongly serrated spine at the front; the edge of the dorsal fin of the goldfish is normally straight or slightly concave. The anal fin has a heavy, serrated spine in front and five or six branched rays. Wild adults may be a foot long and weigh 2 pounds, about the same as the largest members of the domesticated forms. Wild goldfish are native to a band from Siberia and Japan to the Ural Mountains and also are widely introduced into Europe. Today introduced goldfish may be found almost anywhere, including in U.S. lakes and ponds in Australia and New Guinea.

Regardless of the true ancestry of today's goldfish, over the centuries breeders have produced strange and bizarre varieties that they have learned to love. The Japanese, using selective breeding methods, developed many of the most familiar varieties. The goldfish as we know it today can be shaped like a golf ball, have fins that exceed the length of its body, or have eyes that stare upward over fluid-filled bubbles. These features and many more are part and parcel of what makes a fancy goldfish.

Fins

Many people, when thinking of a pet fish, envision a common goldfish. The common goldfish possesses all of the typical fish characteristics: streamlined and scale-covered body, gill covers, large lidless

Though its body form is exaggerated, this Ryukin retains all the fins of a typical goldfish.

eyes, large mouth, and, of course, fins. It is the caudal (tail) fin that shows the greatest variations between varieties. The tail fin may be single as in the wild fish or doubled, one fin over another; the lobes may be pointed, squared, forked, rounded, short, or long.

What Do Fins Do?

The fins of a fish have three main functions: stabilization, braking, and (to some extent) propulsion.

The other fins of a goldfish do not vary a great deal in the fancy varieties. The dorsal fin is of course the fin running down the center of the back. It may be absent in Lionheads and occasionally other varieties. The anal fin is on the lower side of the body, behind the vent. If a goldfish has a double tail fin, it also usually has a double anal fin. The pectoral fins are like hands just behind and below the head, while the pair of pelvic (ventral) fins is on the chest.

Gills

To obtain the necessary oxygen, fish draw water through the mouth, over the delicate gill filaments, and finally pass it out through the opercula or gill covers. This process removes oxygen from the water through fine capillaries in the gill filaments and passes it into the fish's bloodstream. Simultaneously, carbon dioxide is expelled from the bloodstream and discharged into the water passing over the gills. Thus the fish's respiratory wastes are removed from its body into the water.

Nostrils and Lateral Line

Unlike most higher animals, in which the nostrils open internally into the respiratory system, the nostrils of fishes are merely closed pits that house nerve endings used to detect scents in the water. These nerve endings (scent buds) are connected directly to the brain and can detect minute amounts of chemicals in the water.

In goldfish the nostril is a blind sac that serves a sensory function.

Fish possess no external ears, though they do have internal ear canals that serve mostly for a sense of balance rather than hearing in the way that land animals perceive it. To detect noises (actually vibrations) in the water, most fish have a lateral line. This consists of a row of pored scales that runs horizontally from behind the head to the tail base. The pores contain nerve cells (neuromasts) that are connected by a canal that runs under the skin. The neuromasts are connected to the brain by the same cranial nerve that serves the ear in higher vertebrates. The lateral line curves downward in goldfish and usually is not conspicuous.

Pharyngeal Teeth

Like other carps, goldfish have heavy grinding teeth located at the bases of the gills. These pharyngeal teeth, four in number on each side, are situated on a thick, bony arch that is firmly fused to the base of the skull. They allow goldfish to eat a variety of foods, from plants to large insects. There are no true teeth on the lips of a goldfish.

Eyes

The eyes of goldfish are fairly large, lidless, and somewhat movable. Goldfish are generally believed to be nearsighted, but their eyesight seems to be adequate for their needs.

Scales

The body of the goldfish is covered with overlapping scales, which are hard plates set under a thin layer of skin tissue. The size of the

Tunnel Vision

Highly developed goldfish varieties with telescope and bubble eyes have a more restricted field of vision than a normal goldfish.

scales varies with the size and age of the fish. Each variety has a constant number of scales, often related to the shape of the body, the number of scales remaining constant through life. Good scale shape and definition are important in creating the correct body outline.

All goldfish have scales, but some types are erroneously known as "scaleless." On these fish the scales are less conspicuous (transparent) because they lack the layer of reflective guanine pigment that

Growth Rings

As a goldfish grows, each scale grows at its edge. In winter growth slows or stops entirely, so little or no new scale edge is produced. When the water warms up and the fish feeds heavily, rapid growth starts again and a wide new edge is grown on each scale. This slowing down and reacceleration of growth causes rings to form on the scales. The number of rings on each scale can indicate, within limits, the age of the fish, a narrow and wide ring together indicating a year of normal growth.

usually gives them color and texture, a metallic iridescence. The amount of guanine apparent in a fish is at least partially governed by inheritance and also partially due to the diet. Goldfish that do not have much guanine in their scales are known as "matt" fish, while those with a good supply of guanine are termed "metallic." Goldfish with a combination of metallic and matt scales are called "nacreous" (with a mother of pearl sheen).

Color Changes

Coloration in goldfish is due to the presence of black, red, and yellow pigments as well as reflective colorless (white) areas. Most goldfish hatch with the dark olive to blackish protective coloration similar to their relative the Crucian carp, but at 60 days of age they usually begin to change colors. The scales blacken and then begin to fade, starting at the belly and progressing upward toward the back. When the fish have completed this phase, they usually are yellow in color, but with time this color intensifies, giving them once more a darker golden appearance.

Goldfish lack true teeth in the jaws but instead have strong grinding teeth in the throat.

Most goldfish start life as olive to blackish young that gradually become more colorful with age.

Not all goldfish varieties undergo this decoloration. Some may never change colors, staying blackish or bronzy, while others may not change until they are several years old. The ultimate color of a goldfish is strongly influenced by its diet and the chemical composition of the water in which it is grown, as well as its genetics.

Matts are Different

Matt fish don't change colors like other goldfish. They hatch pale (often white) and gradually darken with age as their colors intensify.

Breeding

After you've had goldfish for a while, you might notice that some are getting quite heavy, with swollen abdomens. This might seem odd, since they all are eating the same things in the same amounts. It is

Quick & Easy Goldfish Care

likely that the heavy fish are females filling with eggs (roe). This usually occurs in early spring, just before the start of the breeding season. A closer look at the more slender fish should reveal at least some to have small white pimples (called pearl organs or breeding tubercles) on the head and gill covers. These appear only on males before the breeding season and disappear after spawning is over. Other than these distinctions, it is practically impossible to sex goldfish when they are not in spawning condition.

Spawning tends to occur after rains or distinct increases in water temperature. When the temperature goes from a wintery 50°F to a springy 65°F, spawning may begin. Spawning beds of dense clusters

Female goldfish develop very swollen abdomens that help distinguish them from males, but this may be hard to see in Lionheads and Ryukins.

of myriophyllum or elodea should be in place and the water should have been changed and be very clean.

The eggs are adhesive, produced by the thousands, and may cover the spawning beds. When the adults are removed, the water in the pool is drawn down to just a few inches to cause fewer problems for the hatchlings. If you wish, you could take some of the plants containing attached eggs and move them to an aquarium for further raising. After all, you will have thousands of fry, and you will have room for only a few in your aquarium, so most will have to be culled at some point anyway.

Hatching starts in eight or nine days at 65°F. For the first three days or so the fry just hang from the plants, feeding on the contents of their yolk sacs and not moving. They begin to swim freely when three days old and then must be fed. Natural foods include single-celled algae, protozoans, and rotifers, foods almost too tiny for the human eye to see. When seven days old the goldfish are big enough to take daphnia or copepods or newly hatched brine shrimp. After another 15 days or so on this diet, they can take mosquito larvae, chopped earthworms, and tubifex worms.

Goldfish are sexually mature at six to eight months of age and usually breed when a year old. Since goldfish commonly live 20 years, you will have plenty of chances to breed your fish.

Emergency Food

If there are not enough natural foods in the water of the pool or aquarium, the fry can be fed on hardboiled egg yolks mashed through fine cheesecloth. Mix the yolk in water until it is a deep yellow color, and then spread the suspension over the pool.

Goldfish in the Aquarium

Yes, the title of this chapter is correct—in the AQUARIUM, not the goldfish bowl! Because a bowl just cannot have sufficient surface area to allow proper exchange of oxygen and carbon dioxide so the goldfish can breathe correctly, you should not keep even a single small goldfish pet in a bowl. Always use an aquarium, even a small one, which provides a large surface area and allows you to attach filters and pumps as needed.

Your goldfish aquarium should be purchased, set up, and the water aged and conditioned before you buy the fish. In order to purchase the right aquarium, you should have some idea of the kind and number of goldfish you want to buy. Let's take a look at the basic equipment you should have to keep your goldfish alive and healthy for a decade or more.

The Aquarium

The simplest course is to purchase a standard rectangular aquarium. Other shapes, including pentagons and hexagons, now are widely available, and there is nothing wrong with them, as long as they provide sufficient surface area. Unfortunately, many oddly shaped aquaria are very tall, so there is relatively little surface area in proportion to the total volume of the tank. This means you will not be able to keep many goldfish in a tall tank even with a large volume. To properly keep a one-inch goldfish you need at least a gallon of water with a surface area of 70 to 90 square inches (basically 7 x 10 to 7 x 12 inches).

A rectangular aquarium has the same surface area at the center (when the water level is low) as at the top. Maximum air-water interface is important because most of the oxygen in the water is absorbed at the surface. By restricting the surface area, as with a bowl, there will not be enough oxygen in the water for the fish to breathe properly. A large surface area also is important to the goldfish because it allows a greater amount of carbon dioxide to be expelled from the water. Excessive carbon dioxide levels in the water will cause the fish to suffocate.

While a one-inch goldfish can be kept in a one-gallon aquarium, that does not necessarily mean that you can keep one 10-inch goldfish in a 10-gallon aquarium. The amount of oxygen a fish uses is

They Grow!

Remember that your goldfish will grow rapidly and will not be an inch long for very long, so you should plan on a larger aquarium to start.

Be sure get a tank large enough to allow your goldfish to grow and swim.

determined by its weight, not its length. A 10-inch goldfish weighs much more than ten times as much as a one-inch goldfish because of its greater bulk and girth. If your goldfish are cared for well and fed well, they are going to grow quickly. With a few months of good care, a one-inch goldfish can grow to a length of several inches, so a 10-gallon aquarium would not house ten one-inch goldfish for more than a few weeks.

A 10-gallon aquarium is 20 inches long and 10 inches wide, for a surface area of 200 square inches. This means it could comfortably house about three small goldfish and allow them room to swim and grow—up to the point where they start getting really big. A 5-gallon aquarium can comfortably hold a pair of small goldfish, but a 20-gallon tank that is 30 inches long (20-long style) can hold six goldfish without excessive crowding. Of course, all this assumes that you are doing regular water changes and have a filter running.

Temperature and Water

Goldfish, even the fancy varieties, are coldwater fish, so they do not need heated water. A water temperature of between 65 and 68°F is considered optimal. At temperatures above 80°F goldfish become highly stressed and may die; it becomes difficult for them to get enough oxygen at such high temperatures. When the temperature

Water Conditioners & Chloramines

It is a good idea to keep a bottle of water conditioner on the shelf in case you must do a sudden water change and don't have aged water handy. In some areas the municipal water is treated by adding ammonia as well as chlorine to the water, producing chemicals called chloramines. Aging the water does not remove chloramines, and if your water contains chloramines you must use a water conditioner that removes these chemicals. Such conditioners are available at your pet shop and are quite effective.

drops below 50°F the fish become lethargic and should no longer be fed (because they cannot digest the food), but low temperatures such as this will really not harm them.

Low room temperatures (certainly including air conditioning in the summer in most of the US) suit goldfish well, but be sure to avoid sudden changes in temperature. Drastic temperature changes stress goldfish. When their water needs to be changed, make sure the fresh water is at the same temperature as the water being replaced. The best way to do this is to keep a clean plastic bucket of water aging for water changes. This way the temperature of both tank and new water will be the same.

The large surface area of a bucket also allows chlorine to dissipate from treated tap water. The amount of chlorine in most tap water will kill goldfish if it is used directly from the faucet, so the chlorine must be removed. Simply aging the water for 24 hours allows this to happen naturally.

In general, goldfish can adapt to almost any common water hardness and pH, as long as changes are made slowly over a few days. There is a natural tendency for the pH of aquarium water to drop over time and become more acidic. Your routine water changes will prevent this acidification from becoming a problem for your fish. Your life will be easier if you gradually acclimate your fish to the hardness and pH of your local water.

As a part of routine maintenance, a fourth to a third of the aquarium water should be changed weekly. For a small partial change such as this, fresh tap water can be used without worrying too much about chlorine harming your fish. The fresh water will be greatly diluted by the water remaining in your aquarium, so the chlorine will not be concentrated enough to harm the fish. However, it is always a good idea to use aged or conditioned water for any water changes, no matter how small. This becomes a must if your tap water contains chloramines. Remember that the temperature of the new water must be equalized before adding it to the aquarium.

Goldfish are cold water fish, so your tank should not be heated. Keep the temperature between 65 and 68 degrees. (Fred Rosenzweig)

Goldfish in the Aquarium

Aeration

The function of aeration is to agitate the water, which exposes a greater amount of water surface to the atmosphere. This facilitates the absorption of oxygen from the air and the exchange of carbon dioxide and other gaseous wastes from the water. An aerator is simply an apparatus that introduces a regular supply of air into the water through a stream of bubbles. It can be a small piston pump or diaphragm vibrator pump. Both are available in various size ranges, but the piston pump, which is much more powerful than the vibrator, is more expensive as well. A piston pump will produce enough air to operate a number of aquaria at one time. The beginner just needs a vibrator pump, which will be more than adequate for one or two tanks. Vibrator pumps are efficient and relatively inexpensive.

The air pump pushes air into the tank through a plastic airline to which an airstone is attached. Airstones are manufactured from a porous material such as ceramic or wood. Air is forced through the airstone and emerges in the water as continuous streams of tiny bubbles.

Substrate

A 2- to 4-inch layer of gravel (some hobbyists prefer sand) should be placed on the bottom of the aquarium. The gravel will serve to anchor aquarium plants if you use them and will provide a more natural-looking environment for your goldfish. The gravel (or sand) should be fairly fine, about an eighth of an inch in diameter. Coarser gravel will allow uneaten food particles to become trapped in the gravel bed, where they will decay, fouling the water and causing it to become cloudy with harmful, smelly bacteria.

The gravel should be washed before placing it in the tank. This is easily accomplished by putting it into a clean bucket (which has never contained soap or detergent) and running water through it

Gravel is available in many sizes and colors and is an excellent substrate. It also serves as a home for bacteria important in the biological cleansing of the aquarium.

while stirring and sifting. Eventually the water will run out clear, and the gravel is clean. "Prewashed" gravel is seldom clean enough to place directly into the tank.

Be absolutely sure that the gravel you choose is smooth so it doesn't damage the mouths of your fish as they feed on the bottom. Avoid sharp and rough objects of any type in the goldfish aquarium.

You are perfectly free to not have a substrate in the goldfish aquarium. This is the method preferred by many professionals. A bare-bottomed tank makes it easier to conveniently siphon out uneaten

Contrasting Colors

Colored gravels may be used in the goldfish aquarium for variety. Just make sure the gravel is colorfast and will not lose its dye in the water. Most colored gravels manufactured specifically for aquarium use are colorfast. The use of dark gravel such as black, dark green, or dark blue gives goldfish their best appearance. Lighter gravel will give most goldfish a washed-out look.

Another simple filter that works well for most goldfish setups is a corner filter run by a vibrator pump.

food and wastes, making it easier to maintain high water quality. You can reduce reflection from the bottom glass by painting the outside bottom of the tank a dark color with marine paint. Of course, most hobbyists find that goldfish look better and are more interesting against a nice gravel bottom.

Filtration

Unless you plan on performing massive water changes almost every day, a filter is a very necessary piece of equipment for the goldfish tank. Virtually all filters will clear the water by trapping particles of

Keep the Bacteria

When you are cleaning your filter, retain some of the "dirt" as a starter for new tanks. This material is full of nitrifying bacteria that will be continually replenished in the presence of ammonia and nitrites—and any tank with goldfish constantly eating and defecating will have plenty of both.

The Nitrogen Cycle in a Nutshell

Toxic ammonia released by rotting organic materials and fish wastes is converted by bacteria of the genus *Nitrosomonas* to somewhat less toxic nitrites. These then are "eaten" by *Nitrobacter* bacteria and used to produce relatively harmless nitrates that even can be used by growing plants.

dirt (mechanical filtration), but they also should perform a more important biological function. A newly setup aquarium experiences the "new tank syndrome," a condition of elevated ammonia and nitrites, when the fish are first introduced. This is very dangerous for your fish, as both ammonia and nitrites are very toxic. After a filter has been operating in a new tank for four to six weeks, it becomes colonized by bacteria that feed on ammonia and nitrites. These nitrifying bacteria change the toxins into less harmful chemicals. It is to the benefit of all concerned that these bacteria be treated with respect and lovingly cultivated. When rinsing your filter media, use some tank water that you have siphoned out for this purpose. Hot or cold water will kill the bacteria.

Goldfish are "dirty" fish producing much waste that falls into the gravel or dissolves in the water and then must be changed by nitrifying bacteria into a harmless form.

When you start a new tank, there are some things that you can do to get a head start on your nitrifying bacteria. The most common method is to use some gravel or filter dirt from a healthy tank. Alternatively, there are instant bacterial starter cultures available on the market that will seed your filter right away.

Many types of filters are useful in the goldfish aquarium, from simple corner filters to canister filters. You can see a selection of these at any pet shop and check out both their complexity and their prices. All come with instructions on setting up and operating, but you may need some help from the people at your pet shop to get things going smoothly at first. Box filters, which just sit in a corner and serve mostly as mechanical filters run off a small air pump, work well in small tanks with a few goldfish. Many people consider them unsightly, however. Power filters and canister filters use motors to pull water through complex filter media at a rapid clip, filtering the tank contents several times an hour. These filters are good in larger tanks or those that might be a bit overcrowded, but

Your goldfish will do well in a decorative, planted aquarium, but they also will thrive in a carefully maintained, much simpler aquarium.

Quick & Easy Goldfish Care

Artificial plants look good in an aquarium, won't die from lack of light, and won't be eaten by the goldfish.

they can be overkill in a small tank because the strong current can hurt the swimming of some fancy goldfish varieties. Sponge filters clog quickly and are best used in very small containers. Undergravel filters, in which slotted plates are laid under a bed of gravel and completely covering the bottom of the aquarium, are simple to use and inexpensive as they require only a small air pump to operate. They have been used for decades with good success by many beginning aquarists, and they work especially well if you plan on keeping any aquarium plants. A visit to your local pet shop and a discussion with knowledgeable employees should help you in deciding which type of filter to use in your aquarium.

Plants

Your goldfish can do very well without adding live plants to their aquarium, but healthy plants help improve water quality and give the tank a more natural look. Goldfish will nibble on soft-leaved plants, which can be an important part of the diet. Because of this you will not want to add rare and expensive plants to the goldfish

The Best Filter?

There is no simple answer to which filter will work best for you. Traditionally, undergravel filters have worked well, are economical, and look good with goldfish, which don't dig up the bottom. Corner filters work very well but are not in favor at the moment. Canister and power filters probably are more than you need for a small aquarium.

aquarium, but you can use inexpensive plants such as elodea and cabomba. These rapidly growing plants float on the surface and don't need to be anchored. They also don't need special lighting. Rooted plants such as vallisneria and sword plants can be added after the tank is established and doing well. Java fern looks great, is practically inedible, and grows rapidly under low light conditions when just tied to a piece of rock or driftwood. Of course, plastic plants can look just as good as real plants, never need special lighting, and can be taken out and cleaned if they become covered with algae. The goldfish will not really care.

Plants and Light

If you buy living plants, get only those that thrive under low light levels. Plants that need bright lighting cause problems in goldfish aquaria because they need special lights that will overheat the tank. Goldfish also look best in subdued light.

Feeding & Maintenance

Once your aquarium is set up and doing well, you will find that you cannot just let it go on by itself. Even the best aquarium needs daily and periodic maintenance to keep it healthy and looking good, and of course the fish must be fed daily. A goldfish aquarium is never dull and needs your attention every day.

Feeding Goldfish

One of the most frequent causes of premature goldfish death is incorrect feeding. Overfeeding is one of the beginner's worst errors and is something that many people just cannot resist doing. Fish eat far less than you might expect, and if they are given more

Do not overfeed your goldfish. Feed only what can be consumed in about two or three minutes.

than they can immediately use, the food sinks to the bottom and pollutes the water. Goldfish foods must be easy to find and swallow. Avoid using either very small or too large food particles.

If possible, your fish should be fed about the same time each day, usually once in the morning and once in the evening. The food should always be placed in the same spot, and the fish will soon learn to anticipate feeding time. Goldfish always seem hungry and will beg any time you pass the aquarium, but you must never overfeed. Feed only what they can finish in two or three minutes, twice a day.

If for any reason a feeding must be missed, this won't cause a problem. Most goldfish can live quite well for three or four weeks without being fed, assuming they are healthy and water conditions are good. During this time they may nibble on plants and algae growing in the tank. Of course, you should always try to stay on your feeding schedule.

Quick & Easy Goldfish Care

Vacation Feeding

If a friend must feed your goldfish, be sure to place each meal in a separate, labeled plastic bag and tell your friend to never, ever feed more than one bag a meal. Fib a little and tell him the fish are on a medicated diet and cannot tolerate more medicine than you are giving them in each bag.

Feed a good quality food, never a cheap, bottom-of-the-barrel brand. If it is a dry food, soak it in water for a few minutes to moisten it. Goldfish foods come as flakes, granules, and pellets, both floating and sinking. All are equal to the goldfish, which will eat at all levels of the tank.

Goldfish are omnivores—they eat almost anything small enough to swallow from both the plant and animal sides of the menu. In nature they can survive by scraping algae off rocks and plants, also

Try to feed your goldfish at the same time every day. Your pet will become accustomed to the feeding schedule you set.

eating fish eggs (including their own) and insects that land on the surface of the pond or lake. For this reason their diet must include both plant matter and animal matter to be sure that a full spectrum of vitamins and minerals is present.

Dried goldfish foods from the pet shop are generally balanced diets, but be sure they are high in carbohydrates from plants, have a moderate amount of protein (about 15 to 30%), and are low in fat. A variety of foods is important in assuring a balanced diet, so feed more than one brand and form.

Hanging Around

Older goldfish gulp a lot of air when feeding from the surface, which can cause a problem when it is swallowed and may cause the goldfish to hang at the surface. If this becomes a problem, feed sinking foods or at least soak the food before it is fed so it does not stay on the surface.

Frozen and Freeze-Dried Foods

There are many nutritious and wholesome frozen foods available in the freezer of your local pet shop. These may be whole frozen crustaceans such as brine shrimp and grass shrimp, worms such as tubifex, and insect larvae such as bloodworms and glassworms. There also are a number of vegetable and fish combinations that are ideal for goldfish. As usual, be careful not to overfeed. Frozen brine shrimp should be rinsed to remove any salt.

Freeze-dried foods may not be as popular as they once were, but they still are widely available, easy to store and use, and are accepted by goldfish without question. Almost any food that can be fed to a goldfish, from algae to tubifex and bloodworms, can be purchased freeze-dried. Remember that a little freeze-dried food goes a long way once it absorbs water, so it is easy to overfeed.

Quick & Easy Goldfish Care

You may supplement your goldfish's diet with live foods. If you do so, be sure to feed your fish tiny portions.

Live Foods

It is always a good idea to supplement prepared foods with live foods. Brine shrimp (partially grown and adults, rinsed), blood-worms, mosquito larvae, wingless fruitflies, and a variety of other freshwater crustaceans, worms, and insects are available at the pet shop through the year, often seasonally.

Goldfish have been known to live for years on just dry foods, but such fish cannot be compared as far as growth, finnage, and color are concerned with fish fed on a diet supplemented with live foods.

Many household foods can also be used as supplements. Bread crumbs, unsweetened breakfast cereals, bits of boiled potato, shred-

Earthworms

Don't forget that earthworms are one of the most valuable supplements for goldfish. Large goldfish will consume them whole, while smaller fish may need to have them chopped up a bit.

Goldfish produce a lot of waste. Be sure to keep the water clean by using a good filter and making water changes when necessary.

ded spinach, green peas with their skins popped free, minced lean beef, and tiny bits of chicken and liver all can be offered in small quantities and usually are eaten greedily.

Water Changes

Even with a good filtration system, harmful gases and waste substances will build up in the water. Ammonia, nitrites, and nitrates all are harmful to goldfish, and the best way to keep these harmful chemicals at low levels is to change part of the water on a regular schedule.

Siphoning

Siphon hoses work well for water changes and cleaning the bottom. You can buy one with a bulb (self-starting) or just use a simple hose. To keep from sucking in water, submerge the hose so it fills with water, put your thumbs over each end, then lift one end from the water and remove your thumb from the bottom end and then the free end. If the open end is kept lower than the submerged end, water will flow from the tank.

Depending on the tank's population, temperature, filtration, etc., a partial water change of at least 10% and as much as 50% is recommended every week. Goldfish are heavy feeders and produce a lot of waste, enough to overwhelm almost any filter, so water changes are vital for a healthy aquarium. Remember to watch for chlorine and chloramines and to match water temperatures.

Algae

As the tank matures, algae will begin to appear on the glass and other tank surfaces. Algae are a low form of plant life that is easily spread by spores and bits in water and the air. Eventually algae will find their way into your aquarium, where they are nourished by nitrates and phosphates in the water.

Plant Invaders

If you bring in plants from another aquarium or from nature, you surely will introduce algae into your tank. You also will bring in duckweed, a tiny flowering plant that looks like an oval green spot floating on the surface. Duckweed can rapidly overgrow the surface of your aquarium, but it is edible and helps shade out algae.

Bright green algae provide some food for your goldfish, may help oxygenate the water, and help absorb some of the by-products of fish wastes as their food. The main problem with algae is that they grow over inner glass surfaces and make it difficult to see the fish. For a clear view of the fish, algae should be removed from the front of the glass and perhaps from the sides. This can be done with an inexpensive algal scraper available from your pet shop. Because of the benefits to the aquarium and fish of green algae, it's a good idea to leave some of the algae in the tank, such as on the back glass and on rocks. These algae can also help serve as an emergency food supply used by the fish during your vacation or business trips.

Blue-green algae and brown algae are more destructive and seldom are eaten by goldfish. They can be removed by scraping, like green algae, but are better controlled by reducing light levels and the amount of phosphates in the water. Phosphates are reduced by regular water changes, so you can see how everything in the aquarium is cyclic.

Plant Care

Live plants should be inspected often, and any dead and dying leaves or shoots should be removed by pinching them off between the thumb and forefinger. From time to time it may be necessary to prune the plants that have grown too large. Cuttings from elodea, cabomba, and Java fern can be saved for use in other tanks. Hair-like algae should be removed by swirling them around your fingers or by scooping them out.

Mulm

Sediment, called mulm, will build up on the bottom of the aquarium. This mulm consists of decomposed food, dead plant bits, and fish droppings. Some mulm will work its way into the gravel bed and help nourish rooted plants. At every water change, you can use a siphon run along the bottom to help remove excess mulm from the bottom.

General Cleaning

If you have to clean the outside of the aquarium, never use any cleanser containing ammonia, phenol, pine products, or soap. Plain water will clean the glass. If you need more power, white vinegar and water can be used, or you can find a safe cleanser in your pet shop. The underside of the hood will have to be cleaned occasionally. Vinegar is excellent for removing thin mineral deposits. Be sure, of course, that the lights are unplugged when cleaning. Always rinse cleaned areas with water before reassembling.

Goldfish Diseases

I f you've followed the advice in the earlier chapters, you've purchased vibrant, healthy pets from a reputable dealer and have
set up the aquarium correctly. Proper water conditions and a
varied, sufficient diet go a long way in keeping such nice pets in
good condition, but even with the best of care your fish may still
become ill, often from a common and easily cured disease such as
white spot (ich). What do you do now?

Goldfish are hardy and adaptable creatures, and when they suc-
cumb to parasites or infections it is usually because a poor environment has weakened them. It is not the intention of this book
to turn you into a fish pathologist, but you should know what to

What to Look For

Symptoms of illness in goldfish include:
- Loss of appetite
- Sluggish and aimless swimming
- Folded or clamped fins
- Hanging from the surface
- Lying on the bottom
- Slow reactions to disturbances
- Rubbing against surfaces (glancing)
- Loss of luster
- Ragged fins
- Lesions, spots, or bumps
- Bloating or emaciation
- Pale (not healthy red) gills

look for, what caused the disease, and what you can do about it. You don't need to be a professional to recognize that your fish are ill. You can just tell, just by looking. If you pay attention to your pets and know their normal behavior patterns, you will quickly see small changes that may be the first warnings of diseases.

Fancy goldfish are more vulnerable to disease than are less modified varieties. Fry are exceedingly delicate and are nearly impossible to successfully treat for diseases. If your goldfish exhibits any of the common disease symptoms, consider carefully what may have caused the trouble.

Have there been any new fish or plants added to the aquarium? Has water of questionable purity been added, possibly bringing along parasites? Is there adequate aeration? Are the fish overcrowded? Has their environment been allowed to deteriorate? Have the fish been handled roughly? Has the water been changed without the proper precautions of matching temperature and eliminating chlorine? Have the fish been fed inferior or improper foods, or has the water been polluted by excessive decaying foods? The answers to these questions can provide a clue to what is wrong with your goldfish, and sometimes just correcting the problem can make the illness disappear.

Chemical treatment often is necessary for infectious diseases and parasites. Medications can be given either by applying them directly to an affected area (wound, parasite) or by dissolving a chemical in the water. If the medicine is to be dissolved, be sure that there are no undissolved particles remaining that the fish might eat, which could lead to a disaster. To make sure that there are no undissolved particles of medication, filter the solution through a clean piece of linen before adding it to the water. Most medications purchased in pet shops are already fully dissolved, but be sure to read the instructions just in case you have to remix the solution.

The average hobbyist is well advised to stick with simple medications purchased in the pet shop. These work well and generally are safe if given at indicated dosages. More advanced goldfish hobbyists may prefer to buy bulk chemicals and mix their own formulations, but this is beyond the realm of this book. Be wary of any medication that claims to cure everything.

Isolate Sick Fish

If individual goldfish are showing any disease symptoms, they should be isolated immediately. If the entire aquarium is affected, then large-scale measures must be taken. If the exact trouble is not known, general first aid measures must be taken. A water temperature of at least 60°F must be maintained, adequate aeration must be provided, and only live foods should be fed. The water level should be lowered to 4 to 6 inches so that distressed fish do not have to struggle to reach food and the well-oxygenated surface water.

The Right Water

When the fish is transferred to the hospital tank, as much of its original water as possible should be included to minimize the shock of transfer.

If a new purchase is noted to have sores or you have other doubts about its health, you may want to try to literally disinfect the goldfish. This procedure has its dangers and is stressful, but sometimes it helps, especially in a fish with open sores resulting from parasites or fungus attacks. A strong salt dip is most effective. Try to use water from the fish's present aquarium. The netted fish is dipped into this solution for a minute or so and then immediately transferred to fresh, clean water (without chlorine) in a separate tank. The fish may be stunned for a short time, but it soon will recover. Some of the mucous coating of the body may be shed, but this won't harm a fish being held in isolation.

Be careful with all new purchases. One diseased fish can wipe out your oldest pets, the fish you've had for years. An ounce of prevention is worth a pound of cure, and a quarantine tank serves as that ounce of prevention.

Injuries

Injuries usually are due to rough handling, but vigorous spawning activities, other fish, birds, and insects can also cause them. Injuries

Salt

Non-iodized salt given as a dip often will speed healing of sores and cure minor ills. Use ice cream salt, rock salt, or just plain table salt. A dip can contain salt up to a concentration of one pound per three gallons of water. Long exposures at this strength may kill a goldfish.

This gorgeous Telescope is subject to abrasion, starvation, swim bladder problems, and stress from high temperatures. Know your fish to prevent problems.

that do not cause the immediate death of the fish will usually heal without treatment, but the goldfish should still be protected against infection. The injured fish can be netted out and the wounds dabbed with tincture of iodine or Mercurochrome. A light coating of petroleum jelly can then be smeared over the wounds and the fish should be placed in isolation until it recovers.

Ichthyophthirius

This long-named disease is called ich for short or, just as commonly, white spot. It is a tiny parasitic protozoan that spreads over the fish and looks like someone mistook your fish for French fries, pouring salt all over them. The white specks, actually cysts containing a protozoan, fall off the body of the fish when mature. Then the cysts divide several times into free-swimming cells called swarmers or tomites that look for a fish host to infect. The swarmers can only live about two days without finding a host, so the method for naturally curing the disease is to attack the swarmers.

If you see the small white specks on your goldfish (usually on the fins), you should suspend feeding and raise the tank temperature

Ich looks like white specks on your fish. It may be harder to spot on a white or multicolored fish.

gradually over a period of 48 hours to around 85°F. This speeds up the life cycle of the cyst, thus helping eradicate it. Gradually lower the temperature when the spots are no longer visible and resume your feeding schedule. You may have to repeat this cycle several times until all the swarmers die.

Most pet shops sell several medications for curing ich. These solutions, often based on the chemical malachite green, are effective but must be used exactly according to instructions to work without endangering your goldfish. If the instructions call for repeating the treatment two weeks later, do it even though no white spots are visible.

Where Did Ich Come From?

Most ich is brought into the aquarium from outside. When selecting goldfish, always look for signs of trouble and don't buy anything from a tank with even one fish with ich. Always look carefully at the fins for the characteristic tiny white spots.

Quick & Easy Goldfish Care

Fish Lice

These tiny saucer-shaped parasites (*Argulus*) are very difficult to deal with because they are fairly translucent (thus hard to see) and fasten themselves tightly against the body of the fish. They are free-swimming, flat, round, crustaceans about an eighth of an inch long. They use strong, pointed legs to attach to a fish and then insert a short proboscis through the skin to extract blood and other fluids from the host. Fish lice are most often found on the belly and throat of a goldfish, as well as sometimes at the bases of the fins. These parasites can live up to three days without a host and lay rows of minute eggs on the glass of the aquarium.

Infected goldfish rub themselves against objects in an attempt to scrape the parasites from their bodies. Often they cause more damage to themselves in this manner than the parasites actually cause. Infected areas become inflamed and flushed in color. In a severe attack the fish can become so weak that they die.

If you find fish lice on your aquarium fish, it usually is simple to just remove the parasites individually by pulling them off with tweezers.

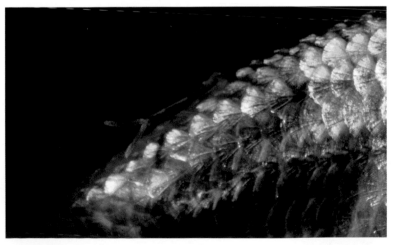

This anchorworm is attached behind the dorsal fin of a goldfish, making it conspicuous.

Goldfish Diseases

Anchor Worms

These large parasitic copepods are easily visible and likely to be seen only on new purchases from ponds. The head bores into the skin of the fish and anchors with fleshy projections; long egg sacs are visible on the skin. You must physically remove anchor worms, as chemicals to kill them are dangerous to use and expensive. Treat the wound with Mercurochrome.

The attachment spot can be dabbed with Mercurochrome (for a large fish removed from the water) or an antibiotic from the pet shop. Medications for fish lice should be available at your pet shop. The treatment must be repeated because eggs are constantly hatching in the aquarium.

Flukes

These worm-like parasites are barely visible to the naked eye, and they can only be suspected until the infestation is severe. Affected fish swim in an erratic and jerky manner and usually appear to be exhausted. The fish may twitch and attempt to scrape the flukes off by rubbing their bodies against objects. The growth of the goldfish will be retarded. In severe cases, flukes (which are nearly transparent, have large suckers at the end of the body, and usually are under an eighth of an inch long) may be visible beneath the gill covers; blood also may be visible on the skin.

Your pet shop should stock a medicine for treating flukes. Usually a mixture of formalin and malachite green, concentrations differ with manufacturer so you must be careful to follow the instructions on the bottle. Repeat the treatment at weekly intervals for three weeks to kill new flukes and also perform a full water change before and after each treatment.

Quick & Easy Goldfish Care

Dropsy

If you took your fish and filled it with air to a point just before an explosion, this would resemble a fish infected with dropsy. Another name for this problem is pinecone disease, because the raised scales give the fish the appearance of a pinecone.

The cause of most dropsy attacks is believed to be a bacterial or viral infection, though poor water quality is the culprit in some cases. It would be advisable to remove an affected fish to a separate quarantine tank, making sure the water conditions there are optimal. It also goes without saying that you must check all the water conditions in your display tank. Check your other fish to make sure none are showing any symptoms of dropsy.

If poor water quality was causing the problem, a fish moved to better water may recover in a few days. If bacteria or viruses are causing the problem, there is really little you can do but keep the dropsical fish separate and see if it recovers naturally. Antibiotics are not effective against viruses and probably will not attack internal bacterial infections.

This fish is suffering from dropsy. Its body is bloated and its scales are protruding.

Swim Bladder Disease (Floating Disease)

You come home one evening and find your favorite Oranda or Ryukin floating at the top of the tank. He is alive but certainly not acting normal. All the other fish are acting as usual, while this guy just hangs around the surface of the water. When feeding time approaches he struggles almost aimlessly to gulp at the food, eventually making his way back to an upper corner of the tank. Every day he seems more and more listless, but there are no outward signs of disease. The water quality is good, but the condition gets worse until the fish is now floating upside-down. What is going on here?

Most likely your pet has what is referred to as swim bladder disease or floating disease. Fancy goldfish are more susceptible to swim bladder problems than are common varieties such as Comets due to their altered body shapes. There are several· factors that can bring about swim bladder disease, including sudden temperature drops, bacterial infections, and genetic disorders. However, the cause is all too often incorrect feeding. Many goldfish owners keep their fish on a staple diet of fish flakes. Many times the flakes fed are the cheapest ones on the market. A constant and continuous diet such as this often leads to constipation.

Blocked intestines can and will interfere with the function of the swim bladder. If this is the case, a cure is easy to produce. First, check your water. Try gradually adding salt (non-iodized) at a rate of one tablespoon per five gallons of water over 12 hours. Fast the fish for four days. (Don't worry; a hungry fish is better than a dead one!) This will enable the fish to clear itself out, and normal function of the swim bladder should return shortly. After the fourth day, resume feeding with live or frozen brine shrimp.

If after this regimen the fish has not recovered, the disease may be genetic. Unfortunately, there is no cure for this and the fish should be destroyed.

Swim Bladders

The swim bladder is an internal organ of goldfish and most other fish, a thin pouch that can be filled with gas to allow the fish to become buoyant and remain floating. The amount of gas in the bladder is regulated by the fish depending on its desire to stay at the top of the water column, hover in the middle, or sink to the bottom.

Euthanasia

If all attempts at treatment for a disease fail and the fish is obviously in great distress and getting worse, no longer feeding and swimming correctly, it is time to think of easing it out of its misery. You may be attached to this fish and consider it a pet, but every relationship has to end sometime. You want to kill the fish as painlessly as possible, and that usually means freezing it. Scoop out the affected fish and wrap it in a wet paper towel. Place the wrapped body in a plastic freezer bag, laying the fish on its side in

Because these gorgeous Lionheads have such shortened bodies, their internal organs, including the swim bladder, are very subject to physical problems.

Gas Bubble Disease

This problem is caused by excessive oxygen or other gases dissolved in the water, usually due to brisk aeration and rampant plant growth together with strong sunlight. The problem is most common in the winter. Air bubbles adhere to the body and fins of the goldfish, which often float on their sides at the surface. This problem can be easily corrected by putting the fish into fresh water that is free of any algae or excessive aeration or by gently agitating the water to release the gases.

the freezer. As the fish freezes, its metabolism slows down, placing it into a comatose state before death. Death is painless or nearly so. Leave the fish in the freezer for a day or more. Then you may dispose of the body in a safe way or, especially if you have small children, you may want to hold a pet funeral for an old friend.

Goldfish Varieties

Goldfish are not limited to those plain little dart-shaped fish you used to see all the time at fairs, carnivals, and department store pet shops. There are a number of varieties, over a hundred according to some experts, that differ in size, shape, color, eye type, fin type, scale type, and other features. While most of these forms can be kept together in a community aquarium, remember that all goldfish are very opportunistic feeders—the more food they can individually scoop up, the more they will. This means that goldfish of varieties with excessively long fins, oddly shaped bodies, and almost non-functional eyes will not be able to compete well against goldfish with more supple bodies and active lifestyles. Comets and Shubunkins grab food more hastily than the deeper-bodied Orandas and Ryukins. Orandas and Ryukins maneuver more adeptly than the slightly less adroit Lionheads and Pearlscales, while Telescope-eyes and Bubble-eyes are the most awkward foragers of all.

While all varieties can exist together in a spacious community, you have to be very careful to make sure every fish is getting enough food.

Shubunkins

These colorful goldfish are similar in shape to the Common, though usually with longer tail fins, which are always single. In the London Shubunkin the scales are nacreous (reflective with a pearly sheen) or matt (almost transparent). The base color is blue, and on this are patches of violet, red, orange, yellow, and brown, with numerous spots of black. At least a quarter of the body should be blue. It is also known as the Calico or Harlequin. The original Calicos were produced in Japan but refined in England. Color in any Shubunkin may take two or more years to become fully established and will

The Shubunkin is the most common goldfish found in the UK. This colorful variety is especially popular in Scotland.

Quick & Easy Goldfish Care

For over 50 years, *Tropical Fish Hobbyist* magazine has been the best source of accurate, fascinating, up-to-the-minute information on the aquarium hobby, from small freshwater tanks to wall-sized reef tanks and even beautifully landscaped garden ponds. Now *TFH* is better than ever, with expert authors and world-class photography sure to educate and entertain hobbyists from beginner to expert month after month.

Call **1-888-859-9034**, fax to **1-888-508-5544**, order at **www.tfh.com**, or mail the **reply card**.

PROMO CODE FB103

SAVE UP TO **63**%

TROPICAL FISH HOBBYIST

❏ 1 year (12 issues) — $28 — *That's $31 off the cover price!*
❏ 2 years (24 issues) — $49 — *That's $69 off the cover price!*
❏ 3 years (36 issues) — $65 — *That's $113 off the cover price!*

(Canada and Mexico add $11 per year. Foreign add $20 per year)

Name_____

Address_____

City/State/Zip_____

Telephone_____

E-mail_____

❏ BILL ME   CHARGE MY: ❏ VISA   ❏ MASTERCARD   ❏ AMEX   ❏ DISCOVER®

Card No._____ Expiration Date_____

Name on card_____

Cardholder's signature_____

FOLD IN HALF & TAPE CLOSED HERE

Excellent Aquariums start with **TROPICAL FISH HOBBYIST**

NO POSTAGE
NECESSARY
IF MAILED
IN THE
UNITED STATES

BUSINESS REPLY MAIL
FIRST-CLASS MAIL   PERMIT NO. 65   NEPTUNE, NJ

TROPICAL FISH HOBBYIST
SUBSCRIPTION DIVISION
P.O. Box 427
Neptune, NJ 07754-9989

The Comet is perhaps the most abundant goldfish in aquaria, but that doesn't mean it is not attractive and worth keeping.

change constantly during this period. Young fish with stunning colors and long, flowing fins may become duller and muddier with age, the fins becoming heavy and out of proportion to the body.

Bristol Shubunkins

Bristol Shubunkins, developed in southwestern England, are similar to London Shubunkins but have much longer caudal fins with very long lobes and usually have the other fins enlarged as well.

Comets

This is by far the most common goldfish seen in shops and ponds. This is the goldfish that is given away at carnivals and such. They also are sold in large numbers as feeders for other carnivorous fishes and reptiles and are bred by the millions on fish farms primarily for this purpose. Millions, however, become pets and live long, happy lives in the aquarium or pond.

Big Fish

Many comets seen in pet shops are small, an inch or so, but the variety grows quickly and can reach 6 to 8 inches in a year. Over a period of several years they can attain a foot in length. At this size they often outgrow their aquaria and may have to be moved to a pond, where they thrive.

The Comet, with its single forked tail fin and rather long, slender caudal peduncle, is an extremely fast fish and aggressive feeder. Young are usually drab olive gray, but as they grow they take on the adult coloration, which may be red (a deep orange), red and white, black, red and black, white, or calico (variegated). It is not advisable to keep Comets with slower, heavy-bodied fancy varieties, which will not be able to compete with the racy Comets.

Fancy Goldfish

For most keepers, all the goldfish varieties other than Commons, Shubunkins, and Comets may be termed "fancy." Some keepers even feel Shubunkins are fancy goldfish because of their colors, though the body shape is unchanged from the ancestral goldfish. It is estimated that there are over 100 varieties of goldfish bred in various parts of the world, but for all practical purposes fewer than a dozen are likely to be found in pet shops, and in many areas only five or six varieties will be seen. The more exotic types will have to be purchased from specialist breeders, while some may be available only from China and Japan.

Goldfish varieties have "standards," written descriptions of the details of body and fin form and color produced by specialists and used to judge them in shows. Unfortunately, the standards vary from society to society and country to country. If you ever get to the point where you are interested in showing your goldfish in competition you will already be aware of the standards used in your area. The following descriptions are all general ones that should help give an idea of the variety when you first encounter it in the shop. Most of these fancy goldfish types have several subtypes or related varieties that differ in minor features.

Don't Get Carried Away

The fancy goldfish varieties vary greatly in cost, and the most exotic often sell for very high prices. Beginners are strongly advised to gain experience with hardy, popular varieties before attempting to keep some of the more ornate types that may require constant dedication to aquarium conditions, feeding, and general care.

Ryukins

One of the most popular yet inexpensive of the fancy goldfish on the market today is the Ryukin. Also known as the Japanese Fantail, the Ryukin is a very hardy variety of goldfish for such a modified

Black Ryukins are very hearty fishes and have beautiful flowing fins. Ryukins are also known as Japanese Fantails.

body and fin form. Long flowing fins are characteristic of the breed and give it a majestic, yet playful appearance. Of all the fancy varieties it is the strongest swimmer and would fare best in pond conditions, though its real home should be the aquarium.

In profile, the body is roughly egg-shaped, the head end sharply distinguished from the body by a slight indentation at the nape (the "neck" behind the head); the head is very blunt when seen from above. Often the back rises steeply from the head to the base of the dorsal fin. The depth of the body should be more than 60% of its length. In this variety both the anal and caudal fins are double, so only the dorsal fin is single. The caudal fin is large and paired, but not excessively lobed; it looks like a fan when viewed from above. The eyes may be normal or projecting (telescoped); telescoping develops when the fish are about six months old.

Ryukins can be found in the full range of goldfish colors, including especially red, red and white, red and black, and calico. They sometimes are bronze or all white.

Veiltails are a variety of Ryukin in which the tail fins are very long and deeply lobed, giving the appearance of a billowy wedding veil. The dorsal fin also may be taller and more erect than in Fantail Ryukins, but otherwise the two types are much the same. If Fantails and Veiltails are interbred, some of the offspring may have single tails, a reversion to plainer varieties. Such single-tailed Ryukins have been called Nymphs and are not considered desirable.

Orandas

One of the largest, most varied breeds of goldfish is the Oranda. While the body of the Oranda is short and high, it is not as stout as in the Ryukin or Lionhead. A good specimen will have nice-sized fins similar to a Ryukin, with a well-developed dorsal fin as well. Like the Lionhead, Orandas sport a spongy, bubbly growth on the head (the wen), though it seldom is as strongly developed as in the Lionhead.

Redcap Orandas are beautiful fish with the red restricted to the top of the head. This color pattern is highly valued in Japan.

Orandas can reach a length of 10 to 12 inches and a body weight of over 2 pounds. This makes for an impressive fish whether in the pond (not suggested) or aquarium. Orandas are offered in a variety of colors, including solid red, red and white, orange-yellow, blue, bronze or chocolate, and calico.

One major color variety of the Oranda has developed quite a following in Japan. This is the Redcap Oranda. It is completely white except for the wen, which is completely red. This contrasting scheme makes for a strikingly brilliant fish. It may vary a bit in body

Beware the Wen!

The wen develops rather late in life in Orandas and is absent from young fish, though you should be able to see at least a hint of the growth in fish several months old. Beware of fish offered for sale as Orandas that lack any trace of the wen!

A young red and white Oranda that shows a good wen and pleasant finnage.

size, fin length, and presence or absence of a dorsal fin (thus over-lapping into Lionhead territory). The red cap has a special signifi-cance to the Japanese, as it is found in a crane that is held sacred. A similar pattern has been developed in koi, where it is known as the Tancho, a name sometimes applied to the goldfish as well.

Oranda vs. Lionhead

Beginning hobbyists often confuse Orandas and Lionheads (Ranchus), which do look remarkably alike in head form and coloration. Just remember that an Oranda has a dorsal fin while Lionheads never have dorsal fins. Some poor Lionheads have a lump on the back, but never a real dorsal fin.

Lionheads or Ranchus

This odd but commonly seen variety of goldfish is characterized by a bubbly head growth or hood called the wen, as in the Oranda. It is a short-bodied, stocky fish somewhat stockier than the Oranda and differing obviously in lacking the dorsal fin. In Japan this vari-ety is especially popular, and fish with very large wens, which may cover the eyes, are greatly respected. The wen continues to grow throughout life, sometimes producing small white pustules that then grow into the warts that expand into the bubbles of the wen. It takes up to three years for the wen to develop fully.

Lionheads have a short, broad double tail that is carried high, slightly above the back, and should be evenly divided on both sides. These are among the most sedentary of the goldfish and are poor swimmers, their stocky bodies and short fins letting them just waddle through the water. The back of a Lionhead should be smooth, rising from the head and sloping toward the tail. Very often you will find less than perfect specimens with bony ridges along the backbone or a low nub where the base of the dorsal fin should be. Such fish should not be purchased.

Lionheads come in the usual variety of colors, especially orange, red, and white in varied combinations. Fish with red wens are especially striking. The scales may be nacreous (pearly) or matt (translucent).

Lionheads are stocky, slow moving fish that come in a variety of colors and color combinations.

Goldfish Varieties

Telescope Varieties

There are three eye types often recognized within the Telescope:

• Spheroid, where the eye resembles a bisected globe attached to the side of the head. The base of the eye protuberance covers almost the entire side of the fish's head. The Black Moor is an example of a spheroid eye.

• Oval, where the oval eye extends further from the head than in the spheroid but with a much smaller base.

• Cone shaped, in which the eye has a large base and extends from the head, tapering to a rounded point protruding from the head.

Eye Types

There are three varieties of goldfish that sport unusual eyes. The eye types occur in a variety of body forms, though most look similar to Ryukins. The dorsal fin may be present or absent. The major eye types are the Telescope-eye, Celestial-eye, and Bubble-eye.

This is an orange and black Telescope-eye. Note how the eyes protrude from the fish's head.

Telescopes

The Telescope-eye derives its name from the bulging tube-shaped appendages coming from the sides of its head into which the eyes are set. The tubes may protrude as much as half an inch from the head.

Typical Telescopes are short, ovular, round-bodied fish that have tails about equal to the length of the body. The eyes must be symmetrical. They occur in all scale types from nacreous and metallic to matt and Pearlscale. Common color varieties include red, red and white, calico, brown, red cap, red and black, and solid black.

Black Moors

This popular and widely recognized variety of the Telescope is a spheroid-eyed fish with the entire body matt black and with relatively long, flowing fins. Very young Moors (because all Moors are black, the common name Black Moor is really redundant) are olive and darken in color with age. High quality specimens usually are a deep charcoal black, but not uncommonly very old specimens begin to turn bronzy. Poor water quality can lead to cataracts in this and all Telescopes.

The Black Moor is a popular Telescope-eye fish. They come in broadtail and fantail varieties.

The Celestial-Eyes seem to be constantly looking up. There are many legends of why the fish's eyes are upturned. They can reach up to nine inches in length.

Celestials

Celestial-eyed goldfish have a rather long, tapered body and lack the dorsal fin (as in the Lionhead). Their large, protruding spheroid eyes are positioned in such a way that they seem to be forever looking upward into the heavens. The upward-looking pupils aid in accentuating this characteristic. The upturned eye is not present at hatching but should be visible in fish four months old or so.

As with many matters of Chinese origin, there lies an attached fable to the development of this variety. One story says that these fish were kept in covered jars with only a slit in the cover. The fish sub-

Celestial Varieties

There are two tail types connected with the Celestial. Those with double tails have medium length finnage with the tail fin about 75% the body length. Those with single forked tails hold the fin high and erect above the body.

sequently turned their eyes upward to seek out the source of light. Another story has it that these fish were purposely developed to honor a Chinese emperor. He found it very appealing to have a fish that always gazed upward upon him whenever he chose to gaze upon them. Of course the upturned eye is a genetic character, a mutation that must have appeared in normal goldfish hundreds of years ago and then been selected for by determined breeders. The eyes of a Celestial will turn upward whether or not they are kept in an aquarium that has opaque sides. Celestials can reach over 9 inches in length and come in all types of red or yellowish orange and white combinations, as well as less colorful combinations. Because a Celestial obviously cannot look downward to find its food, you must carefully check them to be sure they are getting enough to eat. They cannot compete well against almost any other variety.

Bursting the Bubble

Because Bubble-eyes rest on the bottom so often, it is important that the substrate gravel or sand be as smooth as possible in order to avoid damaging or bursting the bubble. Burst bubbles can heal, but they usually are not as symmetrical and as large as the originals.

Bubble-Eyes

There is something genuinely endearing about this variety's strange countenance that appeals to many keepers. Suspended under each eye is a fluid-filled bubble or sac. The eyes themselves are turned upward as in Celestials, and the fish can give the appearance of a little puppy that has just been scolded.

Not unlike the Celestial, the Bubble-eye has a long, torpedo-shaped body and no dorsal fin. The bubble sacs can vary in both size and thickness, and a Chinese variety sports a short body with small, firm

The Bubble-Eye goldfish are best housed in long, large aquariums. Other fish and rough tank bottoms can easily damage the thin bubbles under the eye.

bubbles. Usually, the larger the bubble, the thinner the skin. Larger bubbles often are weighty, forcing the fish to spend much of its time on the floor of the aquarium, resting its bubbles on the gravel bed. Bubble-eyes can reach a length of 8 inches and usually are seen in red, red and white, black, bronze, calico, and blue. If properly cared for, the bubble sacs will continue to grow throughout the fish's life.

Large, long aquaria are recommended for Bubble-eyes, especially to diffuse the current put out by power filters. It is best to avoid any filters with very strong intake/outlet currents (as in many internal power filters) as this can prove to be quite uncomfortable for the Bubble-eye. A smaller than usually recommended power filter set at the extreme end of the aquarium and combined with a sponge filter generally is safe and sufficient. Additional care must be exercised whenever it is necessary to move a Bubble-eye from its tank. Netting should be completely avoided, as should hand scooping. Both can cause damage to the bubbles. Bubble-eyes should be gently guided into a bag or bowl from inside the aquarium.

Quick & Easy Goldfish Care

The Unusual Pom-Pon

This interesting variety never fails to attract attention, though it really differs little from more normal fish of several fancy varieties. From each side of the snout grows a tuft of tissue associated with the nostril (properly called nares in fishes). The tufts are called narial bouquets and are outgrowths of the narial septum, the thin tissue division of each nostril. They vary from a rather small bubble on each side to large growths that overhang the mouth and sway back and forth as the fish swims and opens its mouth. Though the effect is grotesque to some keepers, others find these fish interesting enough to have spread the condition (which is genetic) through various fancy varieties. Thus the normally short, egg-shaped body (rather like a typical Oranda or Lionhead) may have a well-developed dorsal fin or no dorsal fin. The tail fins usually are not excessively developed, so the fish is a fair swimmer and hardy. Pom-pons come in all the standard colors and color combinations.

The unusual-looking Pom-Pon seems to have "pom-pom" projections near its nose.

The Pearlscale is a hardy fish that comes in a variety of colors including solid red, red and white, and even calico.

Pearlscales

One odd scalation variety is different enough that it has been given its own name and status as a fancy variety. This is the Pearlscale. The Pearlscale is similar to the Fantail Ryukin but is distinguished by its scales being raised into domes. The tail fin also is somewhat smaller and has more rounded lobes. The domed scales normally have darker outer edges than the central color, which results in light being reflected in a pearl-like manner. The color range in Pearlscales is wide, including almost any color and combination found in Ryukins, and the scales themselves may be metallic or nacreous. Specimens with matt scalation occur in about a quarter of the offspring resulting from mating two nacreous parents together.

Resources

AquaBid

Buy and sell unique goldfish colors and varieties and other interesting fishes.
www.aquabid.com

Basic Care

For an interesting take on care and other aspects of familiar goldfish, try this site by Russ Taylor.
www.geocities.com/Tokyo/4468/

Goldfish Connection

Want to look at some really expensive and often strange goldfish?
www.goldfishconnection.com

The Goldfish Sanctuary

Almost every type of pet has at least one rescue organization. This one is dedicated to the humane treatment of goldfish and other fish and includes an adoption page.
www.petlibrary.com/goldfish/goldfish.html

Goldfish Society of America

Many goldfish keepers like to join a club. This is the major US club, with many local affiliates through the country and members through the world. Lots of good information, publications, and links.
www.goldfishsociety.org

Health

Does your goldfish have a problem? Check this site for some interesting health information, plus links.
www.koivet.com

PetsForum Group

This is a good place to find bulletin boards and article libraries on many pet-related topics, including goldfish.
petsforum.com/Fishnet

Tropical Fish Hobbyist Magazine

Tropical Fish Hobbyist
P. O. Box 427
Neptune, NJ 07754-9989
www.tfh.com

Usenet groups

These offer lots of pond- and fish-related chat. Give the following a try:
rec.aquaria.freshwater.goldfish
Warning: the Usenet can be confusing and very interactive even on fish-related topics, so read up on Usenet etiquette before joining the fray.

Index

Photo Credits

L. Azoulay: 6, 41
Bede Verlag: 24
Michael Gilroy: 11
Ray Hunziker: 23
O. Lucanus: 47
Aaron Norman: 48, 49, 58, 61

Fred Rosenzweig: 1, 4, 7, 13, 19, 27-29,
31, 32, 35, 39, 40, 45, 51, 53-57, 60
Mark Smith: 12, 15
I. Travares: 17
Bede Verlag: 24

Quick and Easy Goldfish Care